SINGLI

G000152107

MARRIED WOMEN

A Politically Incorrect Comparison

by
Bruce T. Smith
&
Laura Goecke Burns

CCC PUBLICATIONS

Published by

CCC Publications
9725 Lurline Avenue
Chatsworth, CA 91311

Copyright ©1997 Bruce T. Smith & Laura Goecke Burns

All rights reserved by CCC Publications. No part of this book
may be reproduced or transmitted in any form or by any
means, electronic or mechanical, including photo-copying,
recording or by any information storage and retrieval system,
without the written permission of the publisher, except where
permitted by law. For information address:
CCC Publications; 9725 Lurline Avenue,
Newbury Park, CA 91311

Manufactured in the United States of America

Cover ©1997 CCC Publications

Cover/Interior production by Oasis Graphics

ISBN: 0-57644-058-3

If your local U.S. bookstore is out of stock, copies of this book
may be obtained by mailing check or money order for
$5.95 per book (plus $2.75 to cover postage and handling) to:
CCC Publications; 9725 Lurline Avenue, Chatsworth, CA
91311

Pre-Publication Edition - 4 /97
First Printing - 3/98

INTRODUCTION

We REALLY wanted to write a book about the differences between single men and married ones! For example, we wrote, "SINGLE men never remember to put the toilet seat down . . . but MARRIED men, uh, well, they, uh . . ."

Then we tried, "Single men name their body parts . . . but MARRIED men, they . . ." Well, come to think of it, THEY do it, too!

You see what we mean? So, we decided to take a look at the differences between SINGLE women and MARRIED women and we found out there REALLY ARE some distinctions! That's when we asked a few of our friends to come up with some ideas and, well, the rest is contained in this very politically incorrect book.

This book is for MEN and WOMEN alike, So GUYS—this book will help you understand the SINGLE and MARRIED women in your lives. And LADIES—please take no offense . . . Because most of the ideas in this book came from women!

Enjoy!

Single Women . . .
paint their nails.

Married Women . . .
paint their garages.

Single Women . . .
scream passionately,
"Make it hurt!"

Married Women . . .
mumble sleepily,
"Make it quick!"

Single Women . . .
dress to please men.

Married Women . . .
dress to avoid criticism
from other women.

Single Women . . .
flirt with men at
parties.

Married Women . . .
talk to women at
parties and wolf down
the hors d'oeuvres.

Single Women . . .
wear long hair to
entice a man.

Married Women . . .
wear curlers to ward
off a man's advances.

Single Women . . .
say, "Do me, baby!"

Married Women . . .
say, "Go to sleep."

Single Women . . .
say, "Honey, I had a
great orgasm."

Married Women . . .
say, "Honey, the
ceiling needs
repainting.

Single Women . . .
wear stiletto heels to
tease a man.

Married Women . . .
wear sensible flats to
ease their aching
arches.

Single Women . . .
shop at
Victoria's Secret.

Married Women . . .
shop at Sears.

Single Women . . .
say, "God, am I
horny again!"

Married Women . . .
say, "Didn't we do it
last month?"

Single Women . . .
wear tight black
leather skirts.

Married Women . . .
wear fluffy pink
bunny slippers.

Single Women . . .
cook pasta.

Married Women . . .
cook macaroni.

Single Women . . .
never tell a man to
stop drinking.

Married Women . . .
start counting before
he starts.

Single Women . . .
swallow.

Married Women . . .
gag and spit.

Single Women . . .
compete for men.

Married Women . . .
compete for
baby sitters.

Single Women . . .
wear lace to bed.

Married Women . . .
wear flannel.

Single Women . . .
drive
red convertibles.

Married Women . . .
drive
mini-vans.

Single Women . . .
tan easily.

Married Women . . .
burn badly.

Single Women . . .
call the
gynecologist.

Married Women . . .
call the
pediatrician.

Single Women . . .
watch the
Superbowl.

Married Women . . .
watch the
Home Shopping
Network

Single Women . . .
curse openly at bars.

Married Women . . .
pretend to be
embarrassed.

Single Women . . .
say, "A ring
doesn't matter."

Married Women . . .
flaunt their
diamonds.

Single Women . . .
will happily cook
breakfast for a man at
3:00 a.m.

Married Women . . .
say, "Eat some
crackers."

Single Women . . .
never seem to have
periods.

Married Women . . .
never seem to stop
having periods.

Single Women . . .
have careers.

Married Women . . .
have jobs.

Single Women . . .
never mow lawns.

Married Women . . .
do major
landscaping.

Single Women . . .
get down on their
knees to give head.

Married Women . . .
get down on their
knees to clean toilets.

Single Women . . .
buy condoms
in bulk.

Married Women . . .
buy tampons
in bulk.

Single Women . . .
remember their
first orgasm.

Married Women . . .
remember their
first delivery.

Single Women . . .
can't pump gas.

Married Women . . .
can fix a
foreign transmission.

Single Women . . .
stroke their
men.

Married Women . . .
stroke their
cats.

Single Women . . .
wear silk thongs.

Married Women . . .
wear cotton briefs.

Single Women . . .
wear bikinis.

Married Women . . .
wear one-piece.

Single Women . . .
want to stay home
and cuddle.

Married Women . . .
want to be
taken out.

Single Women . . .
give back rubs.

Married Women . . .
want back rubs.

Single Women . . .
buy clothes.

Married Women . . .
buy couches.

Single Women . . .
have lots of
exciting sex.

Married Women . . .
reminisce.

Single Women . . .
take quick
showers.

Married Women . . .
take therapeutic
baths.

Single Women's . . .
purses contain: a
housekey, makeup
and a condom.

Married Women's . . .
purses contain: a wad
of chewing gum,
a used Kleenex and
a socket wrench.

Single Women . . .
know mall hours.

Married Women . . .
know library hours.

Single Women . . .
wear garter belts
with frilly lace.

Married Women . . .
wear support
pantyhose.

Single Women . . .
beckon their lover to
bed for divine sex on
Sunday morning.

Married Women . . .
drag their husbands
to church for divine
inspiration.

Single Women . . .
say to their men,
"I just want to be
alone with YOU."

Married Women . . .
say to their men,
"We're going to my
mother's!"

Single Women . . .
don't wear bras.

Married Women . . .
must.

Single Women . . .
love to
camp out.

Married Women . . .
love to
check in.

Single Women . . .
sip martinis.

Married Women . . .
guzzle anything
handy.

Single Women . . .
love to wear
tight jeans.

Married Women . . .
only wear
sweat pants.

Single Women . . .
want a baby.

Married Women . . .
want their
tubes tied.

Single Women . . .
prefer romantic
weekends for two.

Married Women . . .
pile into the station
wagon with the
family for a trip
to Grandma's.

Single Women . . .
wear designer dresses
purchased in Paris
or Rome.

Married Women . . .
wear souvenir T-shirts
purchased at
GatorWorld

Single Women . . .
read sex novels and
dream of love to be.

Married Women . . .
read romance novels
and wonder where
they went wrong.

Single Women . . .
run 20K marathons.

Married Women . . .
walk the dog around
the block.

Single Women . . .
listen to hard rock
and scream.

Married Women . . .
listen to soft country
and cry.

Single Women . . .
drive like
maniacs.

Married Women . . .
drive like
monks.

Single Women . . .
take exotic voyages
to Club Med.

Married Women . . .
take trips
to the mall.

Single Women . . .
will accept a man
as he is.

Married Women . . .
will accept a man
as soon as he
changes.

Single Women . . .
envy happily
Married Women.

Married Women . . .
despise happy
Single Women.

Single Women . . .
flirt with the
boss.

Married Women . . .
file sexual harassment
charges.

Single Women . . .
buy Playboy for
their men.

Married Women . . .
burn the
Sports Illustrated
"Swimsuit Edition."

Single Women . . .
wear perfume to
attract a male.

Married Women . . .
wear OFF to deter
mosquitoes.

Single Women . . .
watch adult videos
with their man.

Married Women . . .
watch Sesame Street
with their kids.

Single Women . . .
prefer talking with
their men.

Married Women . . .
would rather watch
Wheel of Fortune.

Single Women's . . .
"getaway weekends"
mean marathon
sex.

Married Women's . . .
"getaway weekends"
mean marathon
sleep.

Single Women . . .
splurge.

Married Women . . .
budget.

Single Women . . . chat with their girlfriends.

Married Women . . . talk to their plants.

Single Women's . . .
greatest enemy
is time.

Married Women's . . .
greatest enemy
is gravity.

Single Women . . .
drink cappuccino.

Married Women . . .
drink instant.

Single Women . . .
have posters of
rock stars.

Married Women . . .
have floral prints.

Single Women . . .
go to heavy metal
concerts.

Married Women . . .
go to parent-teacher
conferences.

Single Women . . .
wear tight-fitting black T-shirts and no bra.

Married Women . . .
wear sun dresses and Keds.

Single Women . . .
flash their cute little
tattoos.

Married Women . . .
hide their varicose
veins.

Single Women . . .
wear multiple
earrings.

Married Women . . .
can't find a pair
that matches.

Single Women . . .
have implants.

Married Women . . .
have
mammograms.

Single Women . . .
love to go
shopping.

Married Women . . .
love to go
shopping.

Single Women . . .
use "his" credit card.

Married Women . . .
use their
"allowance."

Single Women . . .
like coffee.

Married Women . . .
require coffee.

Single Women . . .
    drink skim.

Married Women . . .
    drink 2%.

Single Women . . .
read Cosmo.

Married Women . . .
read Cat in the Hat.

Single Women . . .
never say,
"No!"

Married Women . . .
say,
"No, never!"

Single Women . . .
resist their
mothers.

Married Women . . .
resemble their
mothers.

Single Women . . .
are "foot loose and
fancy free."

Married Women . . .
are "foot sore and
fanny falling."

Single Women . . .
couldn't wait to get
out of school.

Married Women . . .
join the PTA.

Single Women . . .
believe in
"till death do us part."

Married Women . . .
view alimony as a
retirement plan.

Single Women . . .
want to "go see
the minister."

Married Women . . .
want to "go see the
counselor."

Single Women . . .
can't bait a hook.

Married Women . . .
can bait, clean
and fry.

Single Women . . .
like an "outdoor" man
who cooks over a
roaring campfire.

Married Women . . .
like a "suburban" man
who barbecues over
a gas grill.

Single Women . . .
hang out in bars.

Married Women . . .
hang out over
their jeans.

Single Women . . .
clean a man's
laundry.

Married Women . . .
clean a man's
wallet.

Single Women . . .
talk "dirty" in bed.

Married Women . . .
talk "draperies"
in bed.

Single Women . . .
go to the grocery
store to meet guys.

Married Women . . .
go to the grocery
store to buy Midol.

Single Women . . .
shave their pubes
weekly.

Married Women . . .
shave their legs...
quarterly.

Single Women . . .
get "smashed."

Married Women . . .
get "tipsy."

Single Women . . .
spend a fortune on
designer clothes.

Married Women . . .
spend their Saturdays
at garage sales.

Single Women . . .
act on the spur of
the moment.

Married Women . . .
schedule everything
months in advance.

Single Women . . .
dig waterbeds.

Married Women . . .
require orthopedic
mattresses.

Single Women . . .
will ask her man to
wear a condom.

Married Women . . .
will demand
that he get
a vasectomy.

Single Women . . .
eat bagels.

Married Women . . .
eat bran.

Single Women . . .
watch big league
games from
box seats.

Married Women . . .
watch little league
and suffer from
"bleacher butt."

Single Women . . .
teach aerobics.

Married Women . . .
take aerobics.

Single Women . . .
pump iron.

Married Women . . .
iron shirts.

Single Women . . .
carry comdoms and
diaphragms.

Married Women . . .
carry coupons
and diapers.

Single Women . . .
live with bikers, rock
stars and jocks.

Married Women . . .
live with mechanics,
plumbers and
dry wallers.

Single Women . . .
wear sheer.

Married Women . . .
wear support.

Single Women . . .
fret about the price
of clothes.

Married Women . . .
worry about the cost
of college.

Single Women . . .
live for the
weekend.

Married Women . . .
live for the
school year.

Single Women . . .
buy vibrators.

Married Women . . .
buy vacuums.

Single Women . . .
think "BYOB" means
"Bring Your
Own Bottle."

Married Women . . .
think "BYOB" means
"Bring Your
Own Baby-sitter."

Single Women . . .
think long hair
is sexy.

Married Women . . .
think bald is
sexy.

Single Women . . .
demand their men
have tight buns.

Married Women . . .
settle for
love handles.

Single Women . . .
collect boyfriends.

Married Women . . .
collect coffee mugs.

Single Women . . .
are on the pill.

Married Women . . .
are on the rag.

Single Women . . .
wear contacts.

Married Women . . .
wear bifocals.

Single Women . . .
highlight their hair to
frame their faces.

Married Women . . .
dye their hair to
hide the gray.

Single Women . . .
get love letters.

Married Women . . .
get junk mail.

Single Women . . .
talk about the best
way to get a man.

Married Women . . .
talk about the
best way to get
out a stain.

Single Women . . .
gain two pounds
between Thanksgiving
and New Year.

Married Women . . .
gain twenty.

Single Women . . .
wear makeup to the
grocery store.

Married Women . . .
go without
showering.

Single Women . . .
sip Perrier.

Married Women . . .
serve Kool-Aid.

Single Women . . .
diet.

Married Women . . .
pretend to.

Single Women . . .
host trendy
cocktail parties.

Married Women . . .
host boring
Tupperware parties.

Single Women . . .
vote.

Married Women . . .
campaign.

Single Women . . .
have big boobs.

Married Women . . .
have big butts.

Single Women . . .
wish they were
married.

Married Women . . .
wish they were
single.

TITLES BY CCC PUBLICATIONS

Retail $4.99

30 – DEAL WITH IT!
40 – DEAL WITH IT!
50 – DEAL WITH IT!
60 – DEAL WITH IT!
OVER THE HILL – DEAL WITH IT!
RETIRED – DEAL WITH IT!
"?" book
POSITIVELY PREGNANT
WHY MEN ARE CLUELESS
CAN SEX IMPROVE YOUR GOLF?
THE COMPLETE BOOGER BOOK
FLYING FUNNIES
MARITAL BLISS & OXYMORONS
THE VERY VERY SEXY ADULT DOT-TO-DOT BOOK
THE DEFINITIVE FART BOOK
THE COMPLETE WIMP'S GUIDE TO SEX
THE CAT OWNER'S SHAPE UP MANUAL
PMS CRAZED: TOUCH ME AND I'LL KILL YOU!
RETIRED: LET THE GAMES BEGIN
THE OFFICE FROM HELL
FOOD & SEX
FITNESS FANATICS
YOUNGER MEN ARE BETTER THAN RETIN-A
BUT OSSIFER, IT'S NOT MY FAULT

Retail $4.95

YOU KNOW YOU'RE AN OLD FART WHEN...
1001 WAYS TO PROCRASTINATE
HORMONES FROM HELL II
SHARING THE ROAD WITH IDIOTS
THE GREATEST ANSWERING MACHINE MESSAGES OF
    ALL TIME
WHAT DO WE DO NOW?? (A Guide For New Parents)
HOW TO TALK YOU WAY OUT OF A TRAFFIC TICKET
THE BOTTOM HALF (How To Spot Incompetent
    Professionals)
LIFE'S MOST EMBARRASSING MOMENTS
HOW TO ENTERTAIN PEOPLE YOU HATE
YOUR GUIDE TO CORPORATE SURVIVAL
THE SUPERIOR PERSON'S GUIDE TO EVERYDAY
    IRRITATIONS
GIFTING RIGHT

Retail $5.95

THE BOOK OF WHITE TRASH
THE ART OF MOONING
GOLFAHOLICS
WHY GOD MAKES BALD GUYS
LOVE DAT CAT
CRINKLED 'N' WRINKLED
SMART COMEBACKS FOR STUPID QUESTIONS
YIKES! IT'S ANOTHER BIRTHDAY
SEX IS A GAME

SEX AND YOUR STARS
SIGNS YOUR SEX LIFE IS DEAD
40 AND HOLDING YOUR OWN
50 AND HOLDING YOUR OWN
MALE BASHING: WOMEN'S FAVORITE PASTIME
THINGS YOU CAN DO WITH A USELESS MAN
MORE THINGS YOU CAN DO WITH A USELESS MAN
THE WORLD'S GREATEST PUT-DOWN LINES
LITTLE INSTRUCTION BOOK OF THE RICH & FAMOUS
WELCOME TO YOUR MIDLIFE CRISIS
GETTING EVEN WITH THE ANSWERING MACHINE
ARE YOU A SPORTS NUT?
MEN ARE PIGS / WOMEN ARE BITCHES
THE BETTER HALF
ARE WE DYSFUNCTIONAL YET?
TECHNOLOGY BYTES!
50 WAYS TO HUSTLE YOUR FRIENDS ($5.99)
HORMONES FROM HELL
HUSBANDS FROM HELL
KILLER BRAS & Other Hazards Of The 50's
IT'S BETTER TO BE OVER THE HILL THAN UNDER IT
HOW TO REALLY PARTY!!!
WORK SUCKS!
THE PEOPLE WATCHER'S FIELD GUIDE
THE UNOFFICIAL WOMEN'S DIVORCE GUIDE
THE ABSOLUTE LAST CHANCE DIET BOOK
FOR MEN ONLY (How To Survive Marriage)
THE UGLY TRUTH ABOUT MEN
NEVER A DULL CARD
THE LITTLE BOOK OF ROMANTIC LIES
THE LITTLE BOOK OF CORPORATE LIES ($6.95)
RED HOT MONOGAMY
    (In Just 60 Seconds A Day) ($6.95)
HOW TO SURVIVE A JEWISH MOTHER ($6.95)
WHY MEN DON'T HAVE A CLUE ($7.99)
LADIES, START YOUR ENGINES! ($7.99)

Retail $3.95

NO HANG-UPS
NO HANG-UPS II
NO HANG-UPS III
HOW TO SUCCEED IN SINGLES BARS
HOW TO GET EVEN WITH YOUR EXES
TOTALLY OUTRAGEOUS BUMPER-SNICKERS ($2.95)

NO HANG-UPS – CASSETTES Retail $5.98

Vol. I:	GENERAL MESSAGES (Female)
Vol. I:	GENERAL MESSAGES (Male)
Vol. II:	BUSINESS MESSAGES (Female)
Vol. II:	BUSINESS MESSAGES (Male)
Vol. III:	'R' RATED MESSAGES (Female)
Vol. III:	'R' RATED MESSAGES (Male)
Vol. IV:	SOUND EFFECTS ONLY
Vol. V:	CELEBRI-TEASE